ISBN 9798721378942

Jasmine Shari
artisticrevoltmgmt@gmail.com
IG: _jasmineshari

Ordering Information:
Quantity sales.
Special discounts are available on quantity purchases by corporations, associations, and others. For details, contact the publisher at the address above.

Orders by U.S. trade bookstores and wholesalers. For details, contact the publisher at the address above.

for
all the women who were forced to forgive
because their
livelihood depended on it...

Why I Chose to Love Again

because I hadn't cried enough
because I didn't give myself permission to break
because the walls that were at one point closing in on me
came crashing down
and I forgot to build them back up again
because space is relative
and the stars may have aligned or
eloped
sending mixed signals in the form of full moons
because retrograde
because I never knew what a first kiss felt like
a second time
from the same person
because the same person who said
they met me in my past life
introduced me to my former self
and promised to save me from heartache
because heartache is so easily forgotten
when you're handed your smile back
because I smiled back
because God recited Corinthians over my soul
before etching your name into the marrow
that would one day become your rib
because your rib didn't fit
so he broke it in two
handed me the other side
and told me to make a wish

This Woman's Worth

I bleed monthly
release pieces of myself that took my mama 300 or so days to create
pieces that could have been my own child
if circumstances weren't circumstances but a conflict of interest
that turned my uterus into a resting place for a wondering soul
pieces that carried that soul home
showing up sometimes as stomach muscles contracting and splitting in half
cause I am always birthing
even when I am not with child
our bodies tend to fold that way
before birth
during birth
after birth
but not after death
after death I am hollow
not barren
because I bleed
but hollow
and there is still blood
and I can't help but to wonder
when is it going to run out
when will I stop loosing pieces of myself

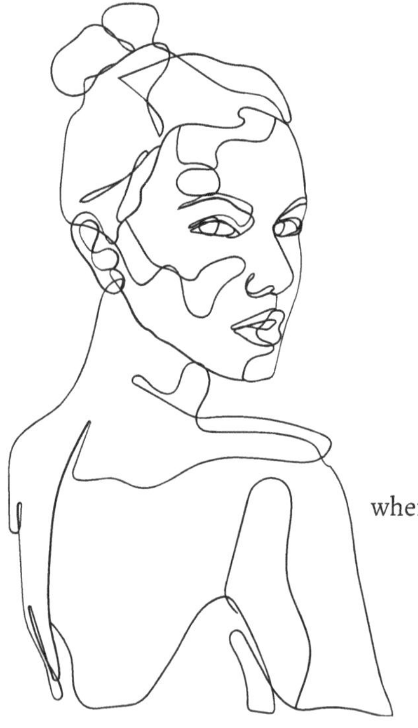

Mama's Cookin

she cooked dinner every night
didn't matter if she was working
she was always working
but there was still dinner on the stove
most nights I never even saw her preparing it… she was swift in her care for us
in a way that gave honor to invisibility
in a way that showed absence as remarkable
maybe it was then that I gave myself permission to be present
because presence perceived isn't the same as just being there
but it was how mama loved us… it is how I love on my babies now because
words fail
sometimes wrapped in obscurity
but if you walk into a home
that smells of hot water cornbread and sun tea all of your worries fall away
they have no place amongst the collard greens
get your elbows off the table   sit up straight   finish all of your food
even when you are full   even if you have no desire to be full
even if you don't like what is being served
eat it any way
because mama made sure we never went hungry and there is honor in that
my table looks a little different
I too cook every night
but we migrate to the living room
the kitchen is a make shift office
my feet planted in front of the stove   wanting to run   but they are planted
and I'm still waiting for the crops
I listen to the rambling of the children as I stir the rice
hearing mama say *"don't stir the rice, let it sit"*
and I can't help but to wonder   how long I've been sitting
contemplating change
accepting these meals
these moments as tradition
not stirring the pot…of rice

Poems

I have had poems in me lately
poems that refuse to come out
because they fear rejection
they sit in the corners of my heart
cupping their knees to their chest
& rocking to the sound of the rain against my face
these poems hold words so powerful
they could change the course of the way you love me
they say that I don't love myself
and
whenever a word forms… tries to inch it's way outside my voice
I swallow it
tastes like pride
feels like guilt going down
I hold onto my chest
hoping to capture the metaphors within the beats of my heart
but they are too rapid
so I become tongue tied
and what should have come out as a poem
shows up as a sigh instead.

Hunger Pains

I cultivated my pride in a dark room that smelled of butter biscuits and gravy
it etched itself from memories of
home cooked meals left on the stove to ponder the abandonment
can't nobody eat a meal alone
this home was built for more than just me
'cept no one is around and I'm starving
so I ate
alone
silent
with only the rumbles in my stomach to keep me company
i ate to quiet the noise
but I didn't get full
my pride wouldn't let me

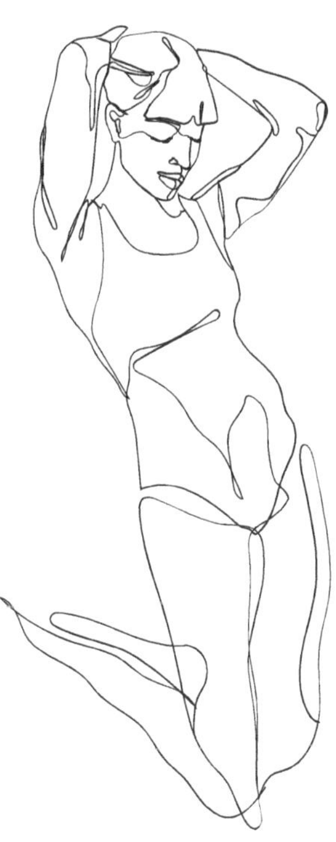

Untitled

I want to have a conversation filled with poetic innuendos... tell me how you metaphorically crave the likeness of my shoulder to a confessional... compare, in simile form, my kiss being as comfortable as conversations between best friends... analyze the way I blush when our eyes connect using a sequence of colloquialisms only the two of us comprehend... and end it all with a euphemism that doesn't hurt but also doesn't have me expecting your return... ill see you again when the tides have turned and loving you is easier.

The Other Woman

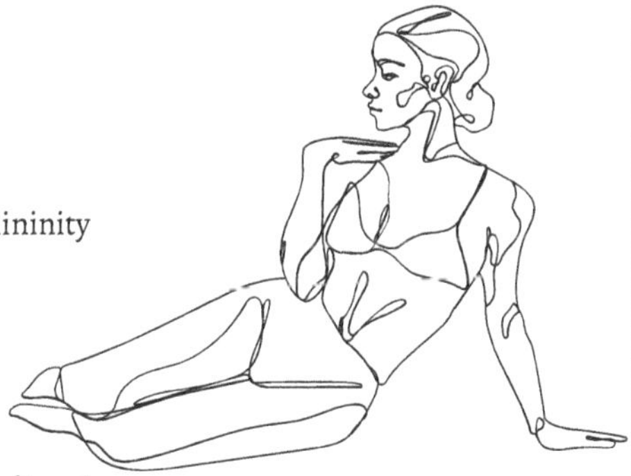

I didn't put my face on her skin
I didn't hang my clothes off her body
my bones didn't break when she bent
our blood didn't leak from the same femininity
we didn't share shelter
yet we occupied the same home
we were not the same woman
yet we somehow loved the same man
so someone was lacking
and for the sake of my future id like to believe it was me
that I married *her* husband
and lived *her* life
releasing him to her
didn't empty my spirit
but rejuvenated my purpose
because the love of my life was waiting on the other side of my mistake

he doesn't speak to me in regret
but affirmation
and his touch is parallel to the feeling I got the very first time I tasted ice cream
refreshing and caused chill bumps on my forearm
I apologized to him the first time we made love
for lending my body to a stranger
for allowing occupancy in my heart
to a person with no intention of ever learning the pulsation of its beat
for being absent
for missing out on the moments when we would learn each other and smile
I apologized to myself for missing out on the smiles
I was in the wrong place at the right time
and intersections didn't exist then
he held my hand though as I crossed roads that bore crucifixes
and we prayed through the resurrection together

Love at First

you know what births sexy...
the tips of fingers gliding against skin
made rough by the world
kisses
filled with empathy against spines
hugs embedded in validation
not for the ego
but the soul
eyes
that shy away from a beautiful smile
during a first encounter
bare shoulders that know nothing of being cold...

Healing

I thought you wanted to break me when I was already broken
but you just wanted to hold onto my soul
match it up to yours
stretch it out
try it on
make sure it fit
imagine if I would have just let you walk away
dust still escalating in the air from the confusion clotted in between conversation
questions left unanswered
and you wondering if the mistake was even yours to be made
you are such an amazing magician
magic so subtle it has fashioned itself as prints on the tips of your fingers
and when you touch me
I disappear into an era where time is merely an intrusion
and waiting doesn't exist
if I never played coy
would you have ever been convinced that a love like this was capable
culpable
past ambivalence
and if I never set aside my fears
I would not have known what it felt like to be loved in patience
it is breathing intuitively for another person
sharing cosmic energy through the filtration of dreams
ti is weighing options
and compromising
and smiles that last past rem
it is the duplication of late night conversations
while falling for each others awkward and calling it love
it is realizing that I was never truly broken
just wandering aimlessly and inadvertantly searching for the mirror image of my soul's song
chich coincidentally sounds like your heartbeat

Unkempt

I didn't comb my hair today
I didn't feel like getting up and getting pretty
I had a hard enough time getting an understanding that my world was about to change
that the very reason I made it this far in the first place had traded me in for a lesser version of myself so
what was the purpose of morphing into myself
I chose instead to allow the strands to run a muck a top my crooked crown
I took my finger and spiraled a coil until it broke off
cradled this piece of hair inside my palm
watched as my tears washed it clean
wondered how many memories would be brought to hell if I burned it
my aunt told us you were supposed to burn dead hair
as not to reap bad luck
and I questioned if my mistake was not setting myself on fire enough for him

I didn't shower
a shower would mean i would rinse away the remnants of our happily ever after and
at this point all I had were the particles left from the lies he spoke which found their way into the crevices of my skin
as it crawled away from him attempting to hide
so I kept the dirt as a safe space
I wanted to keep the feeling of his hand inside of mine
I was afraid that the water would wash away his hold
that the steam would shrink up the I love yous carved out into my palm
until I remembered how often he would cower from affection and the only hand I held was my own
during prayer

I didn't change my clothes
this shirt was the one I wore when I heard her voice on the other end of the phone
saying how much she loved what was mine
these stains are from the tears I tried to fight back but lost to
this hole was from the break of my heart through my body
these rips were from his grasp
I only turned to say goodbye
it stinks
smells like bullshit
but I couldn't find the energy to change it
the energy I needed to remind myself what dirty laundry did to the sanctity of marriage
to the sanity of a person who believed love to be enough

I couldn't comb my hair today
but
when I am ready
when it no longer feels like death
when I can understand that this betrayal had nothing to do with my inability to be presentable
I'll shower and change my clothes
but I'll leave my hair in it's present state of indecisiveness
because it's curls give me something to believe in
that a dead thing
once attached to a growing entity
can still hold structure
on its own

Exorcism

all
of my demons
were
hidden
until
you
kissed them
out
of
me

Love or Something Like it

I want another word for love
I feel like that one has been abused and I don't want to use it
I feel there is too much expectation and not enough effort aligned with its meaning
I feel it's too loose
how many times have you spoken it
what did it feel like coming off your lips into the realm of someone who wasn't me
it couldn't have felt like home
therefore you made it a stranger
and
we know each other
like the tide knows the moon
I gravitate toward you
a calm against the shore
sometimes waves crash
but we don't crash
we don't erode
we don't force what was created before our time
so why would we call it by the same name
love
was always just a filler emotion to me
something to settle into until you settled enough to no longer care that it couldn't
fill the empty spaces
they tell you not to search for a love like that
so why would I call you love
you fill the empty spaces
but with reflections of myself
I see me in your actions
and I have not been loved
at least in the way my father would have had it
so if I'm present
why answer to a name not meant for me
I want another name
like a baptism
we can call it what has protected us this far
what has kept us for one another
maybe Muna (unreachable wishes)
because I had given up on finding you

Belief

this has come to break you
don't let it break you
believe that you are whole
believe that you are magic
believe that you are joy, that you are peace
believe that you are sanctuary

this has come to split you in half
don't let it split you
believe that you are full
believe that you are prosperous
believe that every tear is a wish from a well
and the coins are stars from the sky

believe that you are worthy
that you are fight
that you are burden-less

that your shoulders won't feel much
beside a comforting hand from God

believe that this is not the end
but the beginning
of what most would call

glorious

JMY

had I never known pain
I wouldn't have been able to appreciate your love
had I never felt the pull of regret
I would have never understood reverence
and had I never allowed my heart to break
I would have never been able to say I was loved back whole.

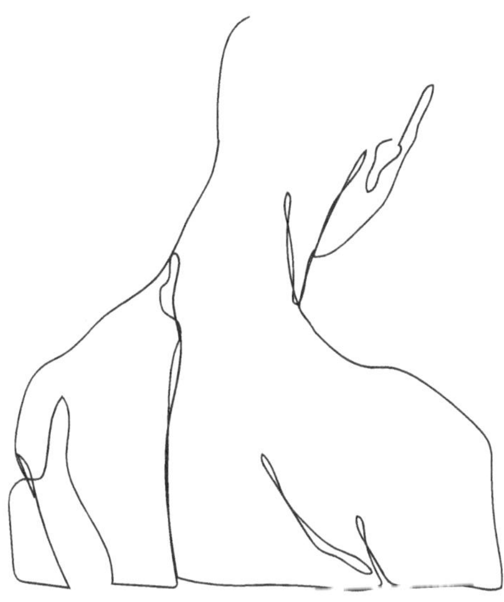

Butterflies

we spoke of butterflies
and how they felt when they settled
but
we never spoke of
the feeling they gave
as they flew away
it's more like a tugging
a burning in your throat
not your stomach
the flutters create a sensation reflective of anxiety
your palms sweat
your heart races
but not from excitement
fear
of starting over
and losing the synchronicity
it once held

Levitate Me

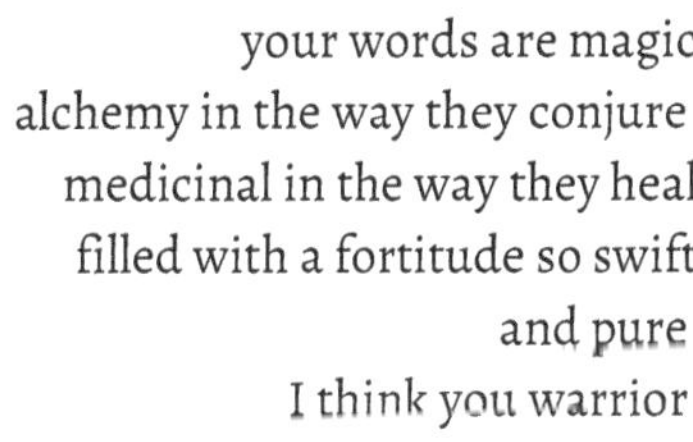

your words are magic
alchemy in the way they conjure
medicinal in the way they heal
filled with a fortitude so swift
and pure
I think you warrior

have we met before
have our souls aligned at a resting place
designed to create symphonic benevolence
only apparent in the melody played out in our voices

have we outlined obedience in the way of introduction
and if so
What were we waiting for

perhaps we've crossed this path a time or two
brushed a shoulder
caught a gaze
met in a dream
so that stranger was a name never fitting for our hello
but a grasp so tight
we comforted the wonder out of worry

is it real
or am I flying
either way, the fear is in the fall
I've never had wings before
so I remained grounded
until today
when you chose to pick me up and spin me 'round
how do you miss a thing
you' never even knew existed...

Interludes

what's love:

him: I love you
her: you don't love me, you're infatuated with me
him: yes…I do… I love you
her: what's love to you
him: when you give a person permission to break your heart but trust them enough not to
her: so love is pain
him: the possibility of pain
her: so you're telling me…it's a strong possibility that you'll hurt me
him: I'm asking you to trust me not to…

Adam

I love him down to his marrow... his melanin... his medium which has become my peace. I love his energy... it supplements what I lost fighting off the ones who never fit his mold in the first place.

The Mrs.

I told him that I missed him
&
no sooner then the words left my lips
I remembered the action
&
realized
it wasn't him I missed
It was the sentiment,
the affection
as far as I was concerned
he could rot in hell

If Divorce Were the Mona Lisa

she couldn't find her Holy Ghost
she didn't fathom it was lost or misplaced but misrepresented
like the bloodshed was substituted for war cries
and the anger varicose veined its way into all four of her chambers
so when her heart beat it was more thunder than melody
melancholy became her pigment
the blush she wore on days her face needed to be painted on because no one
favors a fool with a broken heart
they reek of shame and disappointment
her rouged lips were bitten to keep from crying
the mascara stains weren't stains at all but
sleep deprivation fighting it's way to the surface
they watch her bend in ways a broken woman should never and call her a
gymnast
she would say it's more contortionist than anything
because to fit inside this box of bullshit
and come out all limbs attached
gotta be some sort of magic
gotta be some type of illusion
gotta be a hidden message
inside a cryptic smile
they wrote off as masterpiece

we all have our limits. when you reach yours, you will know. my mistake was
thinking I needed someone else to choose me in order for me to matter...
the moment I decided to choose myself, life & how I dealt with others changed.

if there is ever a choice between you and someone else,
choose you.

-jasmine shari

www.ingramcontent.com/pod-product-compliance
Ingram Content Group UK Ltd.
Pitfield, Milton Keynes, MK11 3LW, UK
UKHW041643190726
13854UKWH00006B/2670

9 798721 378942